Immortal Empresses

Ayesha F Muskaan

ISBN: 979-888986376-2

THIS BOOK IS DEDICATED
TO ALL THE PRODIGIOUS
WOMEN AND GIRLS IN MY
LIFE.ESPECIALLY
INCLUDING MY DARLING MOTHER.

ACKNOWLEDGMENTS

As I publish my debut poetry book, I take the pleasure to thank the Almighty for constantly bestowing his grace on me and surrounding me with genuine and fabulous readers.

I thank my dear readers for perpetually appreciating my writings and uplifting my spirits. Hence, helping me to better myself everyday with their reviews.

I further extend my thanks to my dear family for putting up with my moods and unorganized schedules.

My sincere thanks to Sir Harish Vadgama and Javed Qambrani for reviewing my poems.
Special thanks to author S.A. Santos and Yasmeen for helping me in formatting the book and designing the book cover.

Last but not the least, my heartfelt thanks to my dear best friends' love and support.

My sincere apologies, if I have missed out thanking anyone.

MASTERPIECE

From broken pieces I now became an "Art"
that can now consume the world

POISON

She is pure blend of nectar and poison

She is pure blend of nectar and poison

WILD SHE

So wild, she smokes flowers

I may look serene
But fire reigns within.
My speech is soft
Stop judging me by my looks...
A book is never judged by its cover.

SHE IS LIT

From flowers
To ashes
Back to flames

[I promise to rise high and never settle for
anything less than I deserve and I deserve
nothing but only the best]

BLOOM

She gushes out of the wild storm
Like a flower
That blooms in serenity.

ALL OF MY EMOTIONS ARE PRICELESS

I dwell in every emotion the universe gave birth to…
Including fear and anger.

ULTIMATE SHE

….untamed, free and pure love.

SHE IS PURE LOVE

She is abyss of love
Soaked in sweat of hard work.
Annihilating the tenebrosity,
She built her lighthouse.
Befriending the tranquil waves
She stands alone serene and content.
Away from hypocrisy of mankind,
Preferring to dwell only in what is
Pure and genuine!

WOMANHOOD {ACROSTIC POEM}

Wondrous beauty captivating the earth
Odor of sanity
Made of majestic beauty
A pot full of affection
Never naive
Hand that cares, blesses and builds the world
Ominipresent's love
Obdurate when she chooses
Darling and dare, a divine combination.

BIRTH OF AN AUDACIOUS FAIRYTALE

If fairy tales were real
My burning passion would lie under the blanket
The courage of my soul would be swept under the
sugar coated archetypal norms.
Like a tender leaf that floats away in the strong
mysterious wind.
And my voice would be suppressed with enchanting
kiss of an handsome knight.
My belief too would be just a shadow of unexplained
patriarchy and misogyny.
I feel blessed that fairy-tales don't exist in my life.
As it helps me fly free and be the woman I am!

GRANDMA'S BENIGNANT ADVICE

Her soft tender hands
Ran down my soft lustrous hair.
As she clipped my hairband,
She slowly said "Always be happy
and smiling!"

Words spelled by Nanny were simple, straight and
lucid;
Yet powerful like a bose wave sound touch stereo.
Igniting lava of emotions with touch of fire blaze,
My frozen emotions began erupting like volcano,
abruptly.

I felt Grandma's kisses
Wrapping me from tip of my head to both of my
toes.
All of a sudden,
Cupids seem to be floating in the air,
Carrying a pen dipped in honey
Promising my future shall be bright and sunny.

Grandma's advice, for sure is a bliss.
I imagine without her, how would I exist?
I seal this affirmation on my heart
And begin to collect the pieces of my dear soul fallen
apart.
Philosophies which "The Oxford Book Of Essays"
Couldn't teach me...

Grandma did it in five words and seven seconds.

During summer, when Grandma could walk on embers
And could run bare feet in cold Decembers,
With all her power and might,
From the bottom of her heart, she smiles
And does it right!

I now count my blessings and battles I won
And understand without tribulations life is no fun.

I'm assured if my queen could do it,
I too can, for I'm princess of love
I shall rise in love and fly fearlessly high, like a white dove.

SHE ROSE

She worked like a Trojan
Both during parched summers and chilled winters,
Swallowing the pill of abhor and detest.
She aligned her arrow with focus and
determination,
Sprinkled a bit of faith on her diligent wings.

Within herself, louder than a lion she roared
She soared through the storm,
liberating herself and loved ones from pangs of
penury;
With help of every alphabet she learnt.

Her pen turned into sword
And books into armour.
Her knowledge turned into automated rifle...
She now becomes the militant!
To tarnish the venomous monster of hatred and
injustice forever.

[Indeed, today, she has rescued only herself from the
society and its venom. But this step shall inspire
billions.
This poem is based on real life and is dedicated to
my darling friend
During my college days, she inspired me a lot.
Although she hailed from a poor family, she always
dreamt big and worked constantly in regards to
making her dreams come true. A few of my

classmates mocked at her but she was unstoppable
and today lives a life better than them.
She indirectly made me believe that.. my illness can
never stop me from achieving my dreams)

--- This poem is based on the real life of my friend,
who changed her destiny with the help of
education.}

SHE INSPIRES

In my life's journey of ups and downs
My darling friend played a prominent role.

I rose up from the ashes
Seeing her bloom amidst the chaos.
She became the answer to my questions
As she rose from the destitution.

Apparently, the mystifying picture of her life is
now clear,
And! I take a step further without any fear.

I now assimilated...
Why lotus blooms in murky and filthy swaps.
And why moon is blemished with dark spots like big
lumps.

On seeing my friend rise from darkness towards
light,
I'm assured my future too shall be bright.

These tribulations are just a phase,
I have to pass through..
Just like a moon needs to, before a full moon day.

I FORGIVE MYSELF

I look up to the moon
And wonder how charismatically it blooms.

The wicked dark spots
Fail to erode the beguiling beauty spots.

I wonder, why something so enchanting is dipped in
gray and black moulding??
Yet appears astounding!

I self reflect within myself
After gazing at the moon for a long time like an elf.

The epitome of beauty, is signed with flaw...
I now understand, every beauty does have a flaw.
And it's a nature's law.

Whether it be moon, sky, stars, sea
Birds, animals, reptiles or bees.

I finally acknowledge these flaws aren't flaws
From all of these flaws, we have a divine message to
withdraw.

Hence, I embrace myself, the way I am...
Both in and out, I proudly now call myself a
champ.

SILVANA

KIND YET POWERFUL

Like a delicate snow flake
She captures everyone's heart…
Through the recherche words she weaves.
Her honesty is metaphor for white snow;
Pure, genuine and unadulterated.
Her beauty blossoms in every season
For she never dipped herself in artificial reason.
Every footprint of hers leaves bonafide of love
Without expectations, she spreads her radiant wings
of sparkling love...
Imprinted in her seal, like an alluring white dove.

[This poem is dedicated to my dear friend who is also
an author and has supported me unconditionally]

TO MY TEENAGE SELF

I wish to say this to my teenage self,
"You're accomplished, ravishing and need no help!

You're determined, gorgeous, kind
And almost perfect like a red glass of wine.

When you are love, why do you care for FB likes?
To look and feel good, do you really need
someone else's advice?

Instagram isn't the parameter to judge your success.

A pretentious place, filled with glam, cuss words and
sprinkle of truth.
Shouldn't limit your progress.

Do you really care about the YouTube views?
Darling! Do you know about the light in you?
I wish you had some clue.

LinkedIn might fall at your feet,
If you knew how to deal with statistics.

Your potential can't be reduced to social media apps,
When you shine, the whole world will clap."

SHYAMALA THE BLACK WOMAN

I know a black woman
Whose soul is formed from dew drops of river
Ganges
Her speech is metaphor for Gayatri Mantra
Filled with wisdom, enlightenment and pure bliss.
Her art is immensely inspired by goddess Saraswati
Bringing peace to distorted humanity
And adding beauty to femininity.
Her heart is dipped in graceful bowl
Of goddess Laxmi's blessings;
A true philanthropist, she is…
Spreading joy in everyone's life
With a graceful smile...
Yet powerful like Kali,
Protecting loved ones from the monsters and
sheltering the needy.

THE HAIRDRESSER

As she gracefully moves her delicate fingers
Through coarse, bushy and tangled hair of her
clients...
They leisurely recline on the chair
Submitting themselves in her trustworthy hands
Filled with utmost care.
While she patiently loosens the tangles;
Understanding the anxiety behind the messed up
bun.
She hears the client's tales of both sorrow and fun.
With her devoted empathetic ear, generous heart
And dedicated artistic hands...
She creates a timeless art out of a person
And makes them feel as worthy as Grecian urn.
Ah! Finally the holistic therapy has been done
With deep love and concern.

THE BENEVOLENT WIDOW

Her heart is made up of sun, moon and the stars.
She is genuine synonym for love, warmth and
affection.
Like the sun, her heart contains 2.5 trillion tons of
gold
Enough to fill Earth's oceans and more.
She shines like a diamond, bringing light to
everyone's life.
Indeed delicate and feminine she is…
But not fragile!
She is pearl of wisdom
A woman who knows to shoot an arrow.
She wears the crown made of gold and rubies.
Very smoothly; she handles finances and babies.
I passionately admire her devoted heart
Which beats every second for her beloved.
Although it has been thirteen years
Since his departure from this egomaniacal
world
But I'm assured, his soul now resides with hers.

[This poem is dedicated to my aunt, who is wife of
my most favourite uncle… as per the world was…]

MY BEST FRIEND

She is Farah
A perfect synonym for bliss, joy and celebrating life.
Her heart is an ocean filled with benevolent care and
unfeigned love.
She follows the footsteps of Bibi Amina and Bibi
Zainab.
Graceful talk
Stupendous etiquettes
Immense believer, nurturer and nourisher she is...
As she protects her loved ones with utmost grace
Although, she bleeds deep red.
But smiles like she has won the crown...
On noticing loved ones being happy and safe.
At times, her words might not be soft but bitter
medicine cures you better and fast.
Her every bit of cell is dipped in essence of
mother's love,
Which she showers over the world.
Yet, down below she is powerful
Like Leto, Athena and Soteria.

TO EVERY GIRL WHO ASPIRES FOR BELOVED

Oh my girl! Why do you want to be the Cinderella??
When you own complexion like Snow white
And are opinionated like Jasmine??
My dear, you are wise like Bella or might be
even more.
You are a warrior like Mulan and as determined and
hard-working like Tiana.
You are brave like Merida,
You are gorgeous than Ariel, who lives life to the
fullest and you twirl better than her.
And finally when your hair is better than
Rupanzel...
Why do you settle for so less??

[This poem is dedicated to all those girls who are
desperate for insta and FB likes, I just want them to
know that they are love and likes should not bother
them, they should not value themselves less or their
talent... on just one click called like]

23

BE LOVE AND MORE

Why do you reduce yourself to like when you
are love??
When you are a magnificent ocean of talent, love
and knowledge...
Why do you prefer to be a pond?
A pond - that carries only fame
Only for such a little while??
Why prefer so less?? why ??
Honey, when you can be scarlet rose
Why do you want to imitate a lily ??
When you can be Statue of Liberty and the Taj
Mahal...
Why do you feel inferior looking at the poster at the
PVR mall??

TO MINUS ZERO FIGURE

Oh Honey, why do you reduce yourself to a body ?
Something, that shall fade with time
I do agree it's divine.
For your flesh is made up of love and light.

With help of two souls, you have been submerged in worshiping romance for decades. Darling! Graciously embrace every cell of your body, for it's a prayer of love and faith.

Your scar isn't just a beauty mark on your face, But! It's beauty mark for entire universe.

Why do you try seeking validation from those who haven't seen the sunlight??

Hence, how shall they know what is truly bright??
You are Sirus
You are the lilac...
I repeat,
You are unique
You are invincible
You are plan of Almighty
Perfectly made!
So, learn to love yourself more every day, every second.

STRETCH MARKS

Oh my dear sister
Those stretch marks are the most
powerful poetry written on your skin.
How wonderful it is to allow the whole universe to
bloom within your tiny womb??
How immensely gratifying it is, when nature signs
on your prodigious belly??
The bliss of having angels bow down to see the
regal marks of miracle, is one the greatest
pleasure.
They aren't just stretch marks
They are imprints of faith, perseverance, resilience
and truth.
These marks are prayers answered by Almighty
So, my dear, wear them with
All your pride, love and grace.

TO QUEEN ELIZABETH II

Oh Queen, I wish fairy-tales comprehended
snippets from your life.
So every girl would not wait for her charming prince.
Instead would focus on building her own castle And
understand that working hand is better than
Cinderella's magic wand.
I wish, little girls would read more of your life
Thereupon they would understand…
Crown does not come easy
And head that wears crown is never at ease.

SURROGACY

Two generous women
With heart of gold,
And very soon one's heart for few pennies will be
sold.
All in the name of feminism and modernization,
Behind the facade, patriarchy continues to exist.
One is ripping her heart
And enlarging it.
All for beloved's sake.
As part of her breaks knowing the truth,
A part heals on knowing the other woman's truth.
The other woman, who too holds assiduous
heart,
Is stitching broken pieces of her soul.
Slowly closing every window of her heart that
knows to love,
Although her roots and branches will soon be ripped
apart,
But! The part of seed will always grow in her heart.
Although, they might grow apart but their souls will
always remain connected by tender heart.
A decision of subtle patriarchy
A man's obsession for his own blood.
But finally when women hold each-other's
hand,
The child is blessed with double love
And unique bond is made.

Unique and special motherhood forever!

[In this poem, surrogacy is choice of the man and the
biological mother accepts the deal because of
financial issues. This poem is based on real-life story
in India]

TO THE WOMAN WHO WORE MANGALASUTRA

How powerful you look
When you wear the prodigious mangalsutra
Like a goddess walking down the aisle
The golden beam of the locket makes you
Shine immensely bright.
Woah! You appear like the sun
Shining subtly behind the fog
Like a divine light
It's enthralling to see the power you hold
Towards your beloved.
In a world where everyone is so focused on hate.
Darling as you break one stereotype
Don't form another,
All in the name of feminism.
Your love is exceptionally great
Don't reduce it
In order to fit in particular school or tag.

[genuine feminism is all about the choice woman
makes for herself. Whether it is in regards to dressing
up, food, career or anything… including both
personal and professional life.

A woman can wear mangalsutra and still be a
feminist]

TO THE HIJABI AND NON HIJABI GIRL

Oh my girl,
How does a piece of cloth define you?
Your manners run deep down your veins to the
molecules of your skin.
Your aura is immensely magnificent than the blue
sky
And your speech is more profound than the
sound waves of the Arabian Sea.
Your brain possesses better intellect than the
philosopher's book.
Your heart is as pure as the gates of Mecca and
Madina.
Your soul is enriched with duas of sahabas.
But you still seek validation over a piece of cloth??
It's your choice to wear it or not.

NOOR
THE WOMAN WITH LIGHT

As powerful as tigress
She carries heart of gold.
Shines brightest even on the tenebrous night
Soaring like an eagle
Wins all the battles.
Tender, generous, kind she is
Towards the mankind.
Protects better than a father,
Loves with all power and motherly affection,
And guides like a friend.
She is symbol of perfection and signature of
elegance.
You might break down her castle
But then, she will build her own empire!

[This poem is dedicated to my grand aunt who raised
her children in an amazing manner, although being a
single mother]

THE GIRL WHO WAS NEVER LOVED BY HER FATHER

For she was showered with flowers of hate
She learnt to give bouquets of love.
For her father looked at her with venom in his
eyes
She learnt to sympathize with the whole world
Every time, her dear ones pushed her away
She held every needy person close to her heart.
She swam through the tears
Like little mermaid filled with life...
She was begotten by a person filled with apathy
But the world forgot...
Lotus grows in the dirt.

[This poem is dedicated to my dear college friend, unfortunately, she was unable to receive her father's love but then she was always filled with love and care towards everyone, all thanks to her dear mother]

SNEHA

She emerges out as a powerful goddess
Spreading the divine light
On the dais where the Nataraja bestows his blessings
With her sanctified wisdom
As she moves her hands, legs and every cell of the
body performing the devotional mudras,
Spreading love and enlightenment in every heart
that sees her dignified, lucid and dynamic dance.
Dance, she performs with doting and devoted heart
With sagacity, she delivers every step
Which is filled with perfection
Thereon, immortalizing herself in every eye that is
blessed to see her,
At the same time every cubicle of universe too is
immortalized that views her heavenly and saintly
dance.

[This poem is dedicated to my school friend named
Sneha. Sneha already had established her career at a
young age and while I was unwell, most of my friends
believed that I should settle down by getting married
to a rich man but Sneha made me believe in
my potential and has constantly supported me]

PYARI
TO MY DARLING DOMESTIC HELP

She is Pyari
A warrior, a survivor.
Every day, every second fighting the odds of life
With an evergreen smile on her lovely dusky face.
She wears the tattered saree like a royal mantle
Walks like a Queen with her head held high.
Whether it be an aisle or sloppy street

Her crown is always worn perfectly.

Blessed is every home,

Which is fortunate to have Pyari's love
For she treats everyone like her own blood.

MEHRUN
MY DARLING CARETAKER

She is all the synonyms of tender love and care
With all her strength helping the child in despair.
Her tender touch heals all of my wounds and her soft
speech helps me to bloom.
She is an angel in human form at the same time,
powerful like wonder woman to fight the storm.
She is nurturer, guide, teacher and selfless soul
understanding painful stories of all…
Even the ones untold.
Her words are filled with hope and are more
powerful than a prayer.
Her love can encompasses the whole world and heal
it too,
Oh how blessed I am to have such a wonderful
second mom.

[This poem is dedicated to my darling caretaker, who
took care of me in the most beautiful form when I
was hospitalized and was given bed rest at home]

MY NEIGHBOUR AUNT

She is tall, junoesque woman
Wise, truthful and bold.
Honest towards her duties
Sublime in her beauty.
Opens her door hurriedly
When she hears cough of the sick.
Vigilant and agile in her service, she remains
Until her dear neighbour is healed from pain.
Heart of gold
Brain of intellect..
A well balanced soul
Ah! What a rare and precious combination she is.

MY PULCHRITUDINOUS AUNT

She is both teacher and student
Constantly learning every moment
Sagacity, honesty and discipline.
These three words, she keeps on hymning and
repeating.
Seeks strength from the divine source
Gives in hundred percent to every course.
Beseeches justice
Teaches mathematics
Preaches care
Beauty with wisdom, found very rare. Combination
of Margaret Thatcher and Mother Theresa she is.

[This poem is dedicated to my aunt. (father's sister)]

LITTLE WONDER

She is an angelic beauty
Fairy from the heavenly and silver sky.
Dipped in an essence of innocence
Carries a heart of gold
Showers smiles and laughter
Wherever she goes.
A prodigious daughter,
A devoted sister,
A doting aunt,
In this stern and merciless world
She has developed a heart filled with immense love
and care
Ah! What a beauty
Who knows only to love and serve.

[This poem is dedicated to my youngest cousin
sister]

YOVETTE

Forever young and refreshing soul,
She is filled with immense talent and potential.
Spreading colors and love with her magic brushes,
Which are extraordinarily and exceptionally powerful
And! more magical than the magic wand.
Her colors are true reflection of child's prayer
towards God.
Dipped in gratitude and affection,
She helps the artist explore
The talent and flair
Beyond basic human imagination
With her deep artistic skills.
She helps all understand the divine
And magical and colourful purpose of life!

[Dedicated to my dear friend, whom I consider
to be my drawing and painting teacher]

PARSA

"Simplicity" is her anthem
"High thinking" is her slogan.
With deep passion she pursues
Working for humanity
And! her heart beats loud
For every naive soul
Profound believer in humanity
Seldom seeks materialism,
Strives to love better with every new coming day.
An ardent daughter
And exceptional human
Always filled with youthful spirit.

CHAITRA

42

A genuine supporter of budding talent
Living every moment
With deep love and youthful grace
She cooks the best,
Whether it be spicy dish or home made cake.
A cordial and romantic wife
A meticulous sister and friend.
Once she holds your hand
She never leaves
And goodness in all
Is all she believes.

[This poem is dedicated to my school friend named
Chaitra, who has always supported my art (both
novels and poetry)]

PRIYANKA

She is an ocean of innocence
A universe filled with profound love
She is whisper from God
For those filled with hypocrisy and mediocrity
She is a rose surrounded by thorns.
And a garden filled with rose petals
For those who know to love even a bit.
Tender like flower,
Innocent like child,
Heart filled with magnificent hope,
She believes every person is born to love;
Loves even those who throw stones at her.
How beautiful it is to know only the subject of
love??
In a world where power, prejudice, hypocrisy
And words like lust and money trend.

[This poem is again dedicated to my school friend
named Priyanka. Although, her brain is slightly
deficient but her power to love everyone makes me
speechless]

SHIVALI

Symbol of Shiva's love
Shivali she is...
Filled with goddess Kali's power and Saraswati's love,
She is a untamed lioness
Spreading love everywhere.
A genuine personification of
Goddess Lakshmi
For her labour never fails.
Love, power, beauty, richness, grace
Ah! How beautifully she balances all.

[This poem is dedicated to my dear friend Shivali.
She is an income tax officer, she has immense love
for art and supports every artist with her
unconditional love]

KULSUM

Like a lioness she protects
her loved ones.
Always ready for any battle
Yet carries the softest heart with deep love.
Submits herself to duty of nurturer
And believes it empowers her!
An empowerment, enough to protect the whole
universe.
A reverential and devoted wife,
Loves even the flaws of her husband with
immense pride.
A conscientious and duteous daughter
Taking colossal care about the needs of her father.
A maven in delivering motherly services
And above all, exceptionally talented
chemistry teacher...
She chooses to love others
Before herself.

[Dedicated to my sister-in-law, who is more like a
sister]

TO ALL OF MY DEAR AUNTS

In the tenebrous night
You enter as the divine light
Calming the chaos of our life.
And with all the beauty you strive
To paint the magnificent colours
On the dull canvas of our life.
Your words create melody
Healing every part of our body.

An alluring therapy,
A blessed raga you are,
Constantly showering blessings and protecting
Like the mother earth.
Life is for sure better with you
Under the shadow of your benevolent love and care.

[This poem is dedicated to all of my dear
aunts… including both aunts, grandaunts.]

TO ALL MY DEAR TEACHERS

Dipped in Saga of consistency
Showering the sparkle of golden wise ragas
resplendently.
Holding the hand of tender talent
They walk with patience, gracefully.
Helping the little seed to bloom to its best
They sacrifice their nest.
Annihilating both night and day
They work relentlessly
And genuinely for every disciple they pray.
They wear the platinum & diamond studded badge
with pride
As they see part of them fly up and far away.

TO ALL OF MY COUSIN SISTERS

Sweet little flowers
Dipped in pure honey
They shine like golden daffodils in my life.
Spreading illuminating happiness
With sparkle of sun rays,
With their love and presence they make my worries
less
And add smiles to my face.
That run ear to ear
As river Nile.
They are shooting stars in my life.
When everything is messed up
They help me in fixing everything right.

TO THE GIRL WITH EPILEPSY

She is a wounded lioness
And more powerful than Artemisia- The Empress
The scars on her petite and vivacious body,
And smile on her heavenly and scintillating lips,
Helps us know
She just won the battle.
As she steps down the aisle with pride,
Her beauty resembles the enchanting bride.
She steadily picks up the fallen arrows
And gracefully sits on the throne.
She is once more vigilant and armed;
On knowing she should soon encounter a storm
again.

TO THE MARRIED AND UNMARRIED GIRL

Dear women,
You don't need arms of a man to approve your
warmth
You neither need the business strategy measure scale
to know your potential or your growth.
Nor you need to be a mother
To bless any child with your motherly love.
This deep intrinsic characteristic which you carry
from your birth.
Believe me ! If the archetypal pattern does not
endorse you

You become no less.
You need no PhD degree to speak about your
experience or your morals or ethics.
None of the labels complete you,
None of the labels destroy you,
None of these labels make you less or more.
For you are born out of the Divine force
Exceptionally powerful and unique
In your own way.
Be you and rise above the stereotypes.

MOM

A few of my poems are incomplete,
To write my thoughts seems an impossible feat,
I am sure this poem is one of those too,
That's got its rhythm all askew.

For every time I utter with love, the word "Maa".
My feelings begin to go Ga Ga!
You are the non-stop walking poetry in my life
Blessed with beauty like that of Aphrodite.
Like a genie in one blow
With your one word and tender touch
You turn my melancholic state into euphoric
heavenly paradise.
In my parallel universe, you are my Alladin's
magic lamp and Glinda's magic wand.
At every step treating me like princess
And making me believe...
Best is all I deserve.
I am amazed at your magical powers
Walking on hot embers you still continue to smile.
A man can definitely not sail in two boats
But a woman can, especially when a mother
At times even in ten.
With your exhausting eyelids, you continue to stay
awake
And fulfill every dear ones dream,
And the power to call them yours,
Is nothing but just divine love.

Unselfish, unadulterated, sacrificing you are
And your morals are dipped in essence of Bibi
Khadija and Bibi Fathima...
I wish I could complete the poem
If I only knew how a mom does all the work with
such ease
And wish I understood, how you love with so much
power ??

TO EVERY GIRL WHO SUPPORTED ME

As I was floating on the dark river
Cumulonimbus and gloomy sunset made me shiver.
Overwhelmed with tenebrosity in my cave,
I could see nothing but twilight stage.
While, my breath had almost come to an end
I heard you calling me – Dear friend!
Like an aurora, creeping into the dark forest
Your kind words made me believe, I was unique and
the best!
As you held my hand, I got back the power and zest.
You told me right on to the face
" A warrior will be put through the test,
And you have to win every race!"
Today, here I stand holding the golden shield
With smile on my lips, I look across the field.
It was your love with which I was able to win the
deal,
My words will always fall short for your support,
kindness and generous appeal.

MOTHER IS A MOTHER

A mother's love is as deep as the ocean
As powerful as the phoenix.
Alike the sun, she burns herself
To protect the child.
And with her enchanting voice
She hums a berceuse,
More soothing than the moonlight.
She constantly keeps protecting, loving and
nurturing
Her sacrifices help the child to bloom into the most
magnificent being.

Well does it matter if the mother is connected by
blood, a stepmom, surrogate or has adopted you?

TO GREAT GRANDMA

Brighter than the moonlight
Filled with sagacity and divine light,
Her white hair tells me a story
Of tenderness and honesty.
Built with fierce love was every cell of hers
Her soft and naive voice was submerged
both in azaan calls and church bells.
As she did utter words of lullaby with grace
My heart skipped a beat,
Oh how impressive she was
Both immensely powerful and generous.
Her heart was made out of most precious and
delicate gems,
This sweet lady believed,
I was born to touch the sky,
As I try walking on her footsteps
I understand
She was born to bring in a revolution
Highly well balanced in personal life, career
and profession,
Never did she try to give justification.
Her actions spoke million words of kindness
How do I explain or write about the lady ??
My goodness!! the Queen of my life says she is
the best!

[Queen here refers to my mom]

The further poems are written by my dear friends who are exceptionally talented poets named Harish Vadgama and Javed Qambrani

I take immense pleasure in publishing their poems and is a small gesture of thanks by my side..as they have always supported and encouraged me.

VAGABOUND

Stranger to the land I had never been,
Where everything was so differently seen.

Where a smile was suspicious,
A simple 'Thank You' even more odious.

Where homes were splattered in mud,
And red windows that looked like painted blood.

I shook my head in despair,
Thinking there was something wrong somewhere.

Was it in my mind I saw these things,
With hideous thoughts flying to all four winds.

I thought I saw torn down doors,,
And lying across wooden floors,

Untidy pairs of shoes scattered and
thrown
Of little children not yet fully grown.

This was a land of people so very queer,
I thought, as I ran back home in downright fear.

BY HARISH V

ARDHANGINI

Once a woman unto myself
I had not heard of sin.

My presence was a gift
I freely gave to him

Yet a stranger's words were clouds
That hid the sun.

"Impure," he said of me
"Half of her husband is she," he said,
"Ardhangini…"

BY HARISH V

INKED

She couldn't escape
She couldn't fight

From clothes to shreds
From days to nights

She stood there naked and shy
She paused and wondered why

She didn't resist but endured
Her Soul was bruised and blood poured

All she wanted was –"to express"

She dared to become a writer
They taught her a good lesson

And Inked the rules on her…
Yes, INKED THE RULES ON HER…

BY HARISH V

AYESHA (AISHA)

IN HONOUR OF AYESHA

Her name's Aisha, she writes, ruling the world of
writeups
She's rising sun world steals light from enough to
light up
Metal bullets are her words sometimes, pen is her
gun
Shooting evil dead when triggered by the conception
Flowers of love are her words sometimes paper's a
garden perfuming the whole world with fragrance of
the passions
Her words serve as soul sometimes, pen as an
injection injecting dead dreams with soul she starts
resurrection

BY JAVED QAMBRANI

MISGONY

Misogyny tends to burn woman's wings

To prevent her soaring in sky of freedom

She breathes air of freedom treading on earth

Seeing her treading the earth to breathe freedom

Misogynists break her limbs to check her move

To desired destination led by freedom

Breaking her limbs fail to hinder her movement

As crawling lets her move on earth of freedom

Translating her dreams into reality

Fire inside her for freedom offsets fire

Set by misogyny to her existence
To make her soul crave for eternal freedom

BY JAVED QAMBRANI

TATTOOS OF OPPRESSION

She's to remove tattoos of oppression from her
soul,
Painted forcibly by artists of misogyny.
She's to reject bronze ornaments of male dominance
Gifted by the biased goldsmiths of male chauvinism.
She ain't bad wife as she gives in-laws access to dot
Of devotion brought by her from the parental home.
Race survives extinction, courtesy of her existence
Donating womb for birth of child irrespective of sex
Achievements are cosmetic surgery she's to have to
remove deprivation scars left by misogynists.
She's to gain control of human rights, patriarchy
annexed.

BY JAVED QAMBRANI

EVE'S DAUGHTER

She's Eve's daughter created from clay
With her emotions made of cool breeze
Blowing from the ocean of her heart
To cool the hot island of my heart,
And with adoration made of water
Flowing in generosity river
To irrigate my soul's barren land
En route to salty sea of my life
To turn its saltiness in sweetness
When two waters mix in estuary

POWERFUL SHE (COLLABORATION)

Girl go hunting, your weapon is the feminism

Designed to hunt fierce beast of misogyny

That lies in wait for you in prejudice jungle
Sure to lose life in feminism controlled hunt

Have arrows of achievements in your quiver

Enough to shoot wolf of male supremacy dead

Girl go hunting with sensible sword of human rights

Before bloodhound of male chauvinism can hunt
you

Girl go setting example for womenfolk

Putting to sword of skills beast of male dominance
Like Razia Sultana who crushed misogynists
To set up invincible reign of feminism.

JAVED QAMBRANI

I am complete woman without a man

As my surname remains witness to it.

I grew up hearing stories of empresses

Told by my dear mother in profound manner

I'm not to be shattered by your stereotypes

When you speak about "he" completing me.

I don't rely on whatever is dust made,

Instead, on Almighty as my Shield .

I have idolized Rabia Basri (R.A), who could tame both lion and the sheep.

More you put strong stories underneath the carpet,

More Ayeshas will take birth to kill misogyny .

BY AYESHA F .MUSKAAN

[A collaboration by Javed Q and me]

ABOUT THE AUTHOR

Ayesha F Muskaan began writing at the age of 6 and successfully published her poems at the age of 19 in the 'Poets International Magazine'. She was born and brought up in Bangalore. She keeps a keen interest in writing, reading, and painting. As a child, her epilepsy refrained her from playing outdoors. Yet she was not discouraged rather took a keen interest in observing nature and applauded its beauty in her poems.

She has worked in three anthologies- Colour My Dreams, We @ 20, and Ecstatic Serenity. She has also volunteered for 'YFS' (Youth For Seva) and Amrutha Bindu. Presently she works as a freelance writer, editor and book reviewer. She has done Masters's in Literature. She is well known on Instagram as @ayesha_f_muskaan where she shares her poetry and thoughts.

Both her novels "Messiah" and "Divine souls" have been among bestsellers. "Immortal empresses" is her debut poetry book.

9 798888 963762